40
VEGETABLES
Kids Coloring Book

NINALARS

This Book Belongs To

CABBAGE

BROCCOLI

EGGPLANT

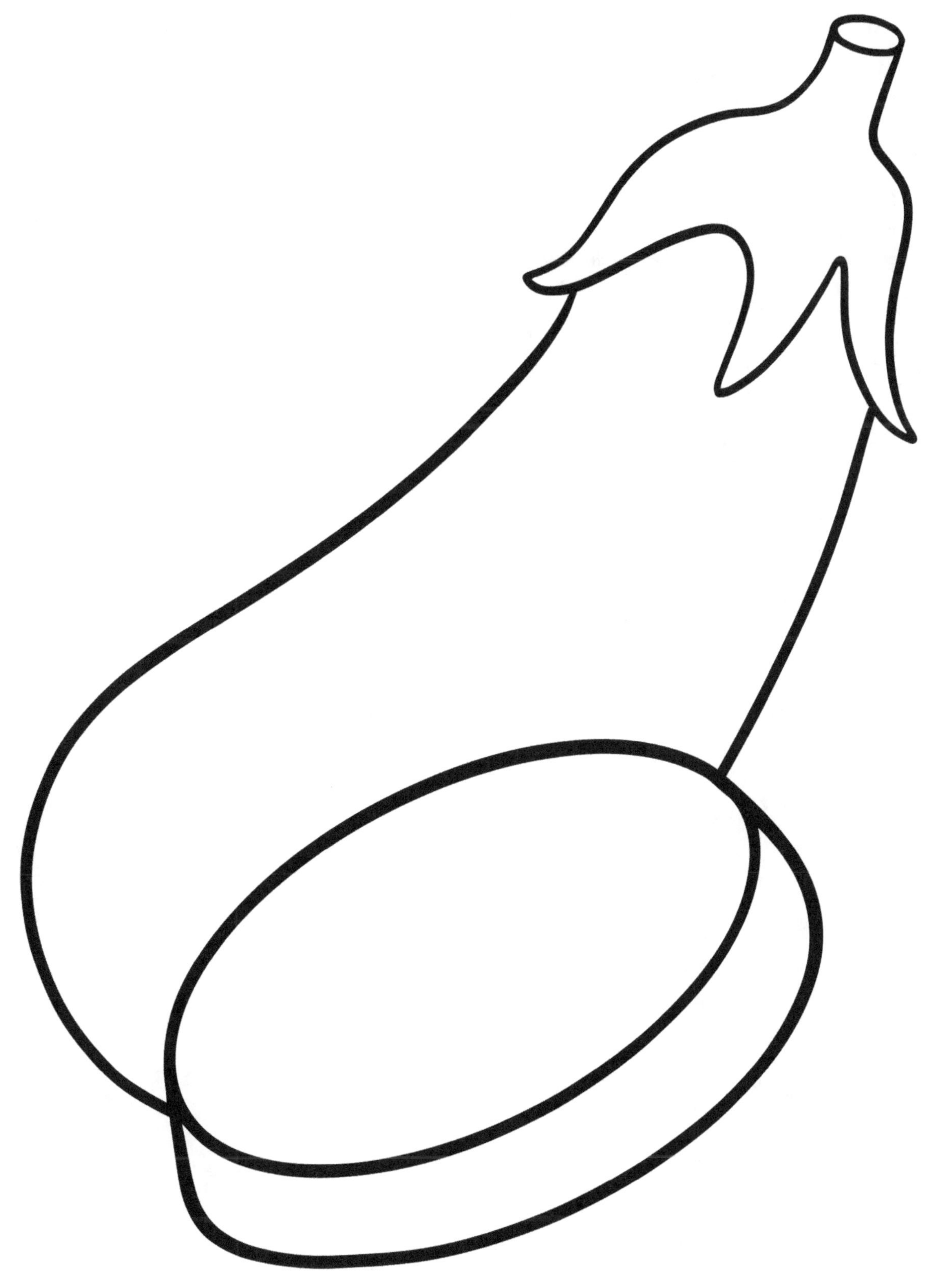

CHILI

JICAMA

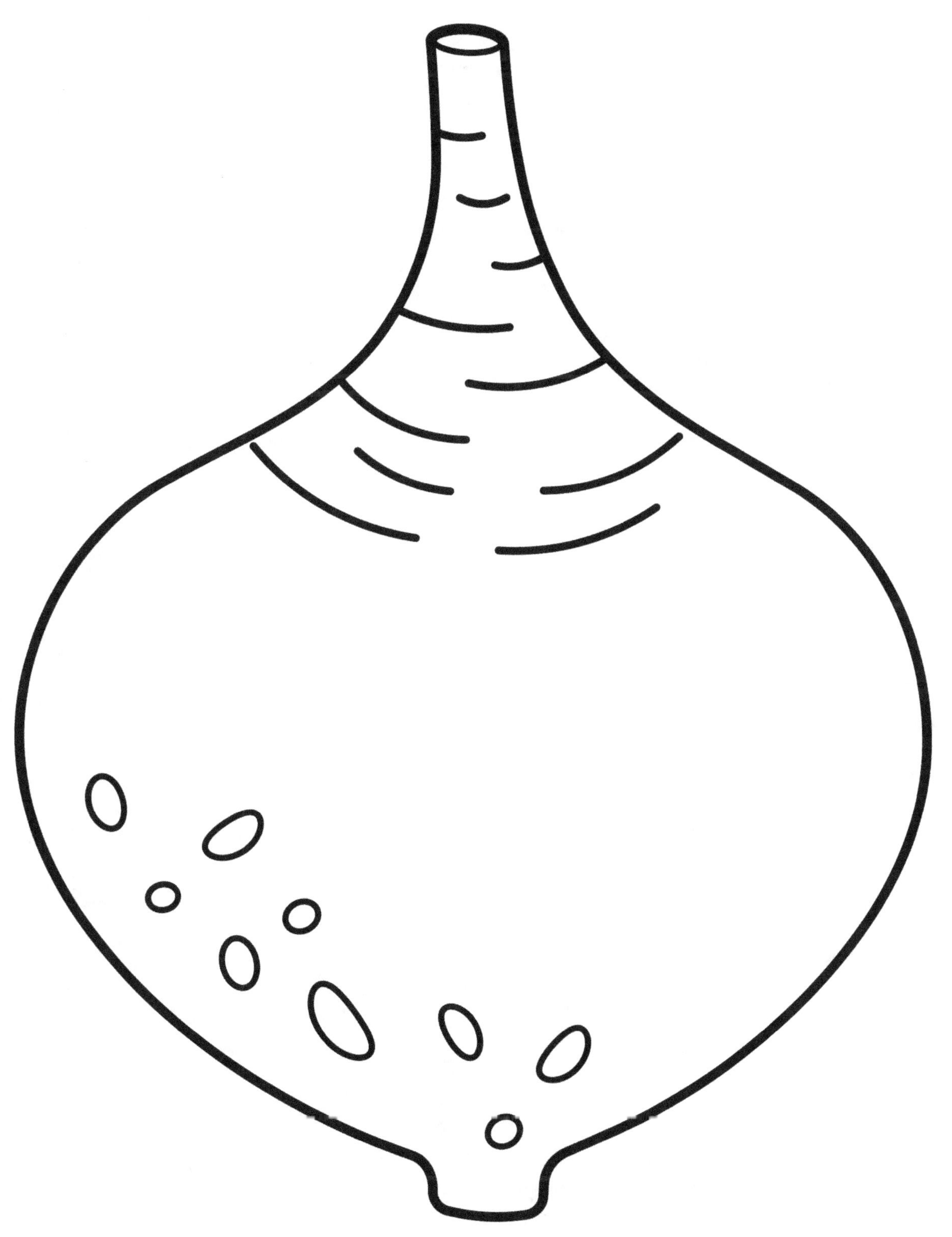

TOMATO

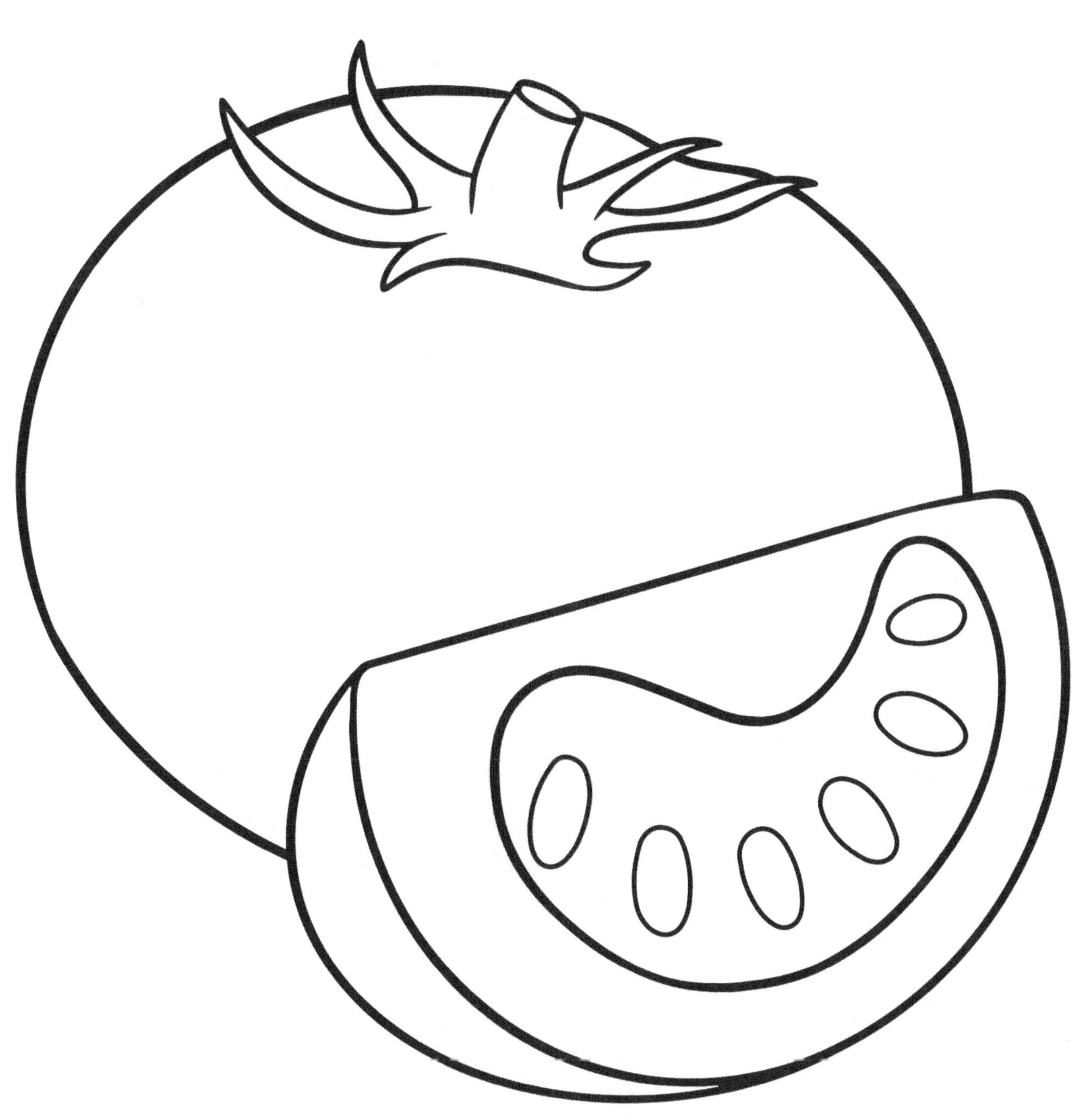

SWEET POTATO

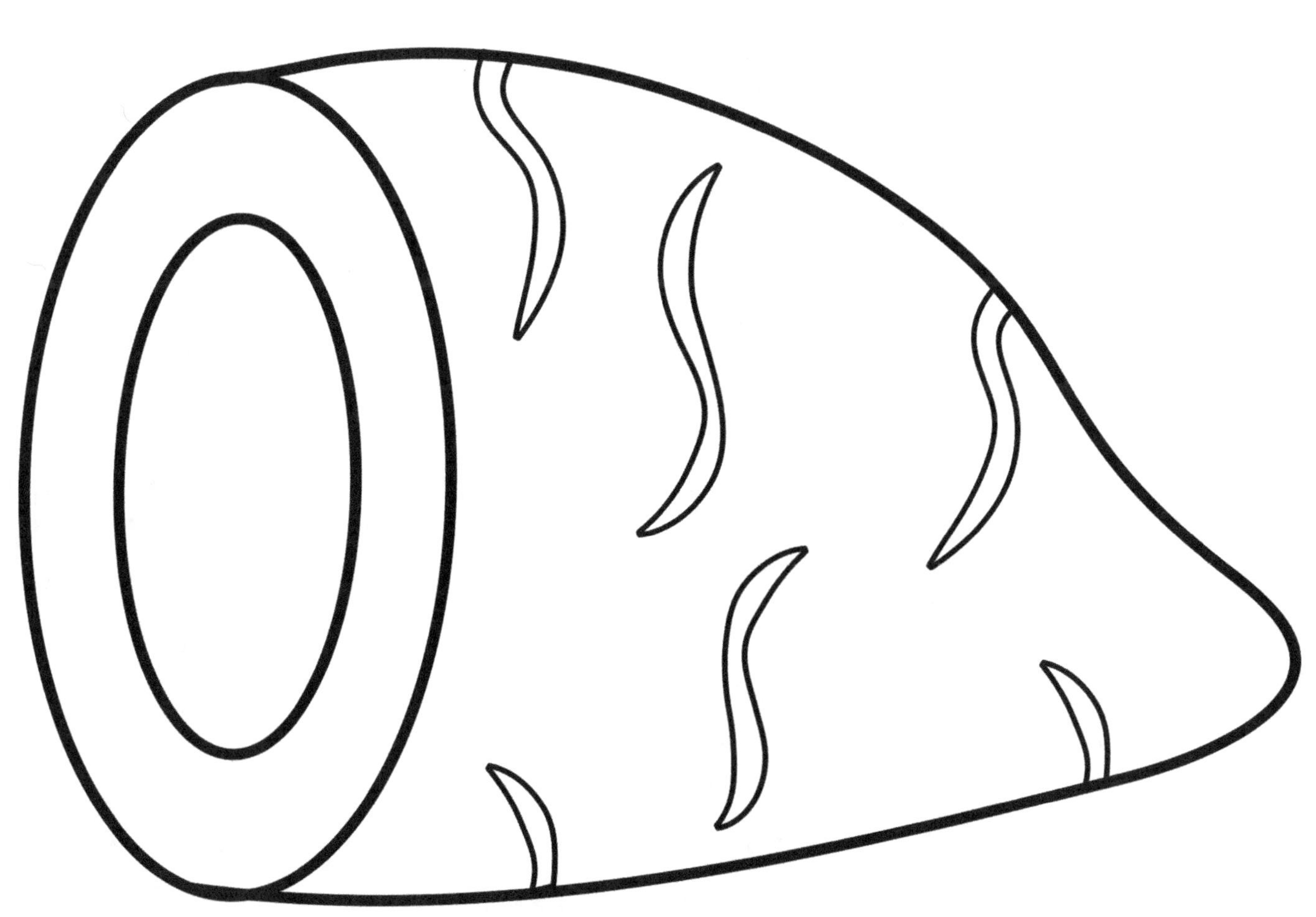

TURNIP

DAIKON

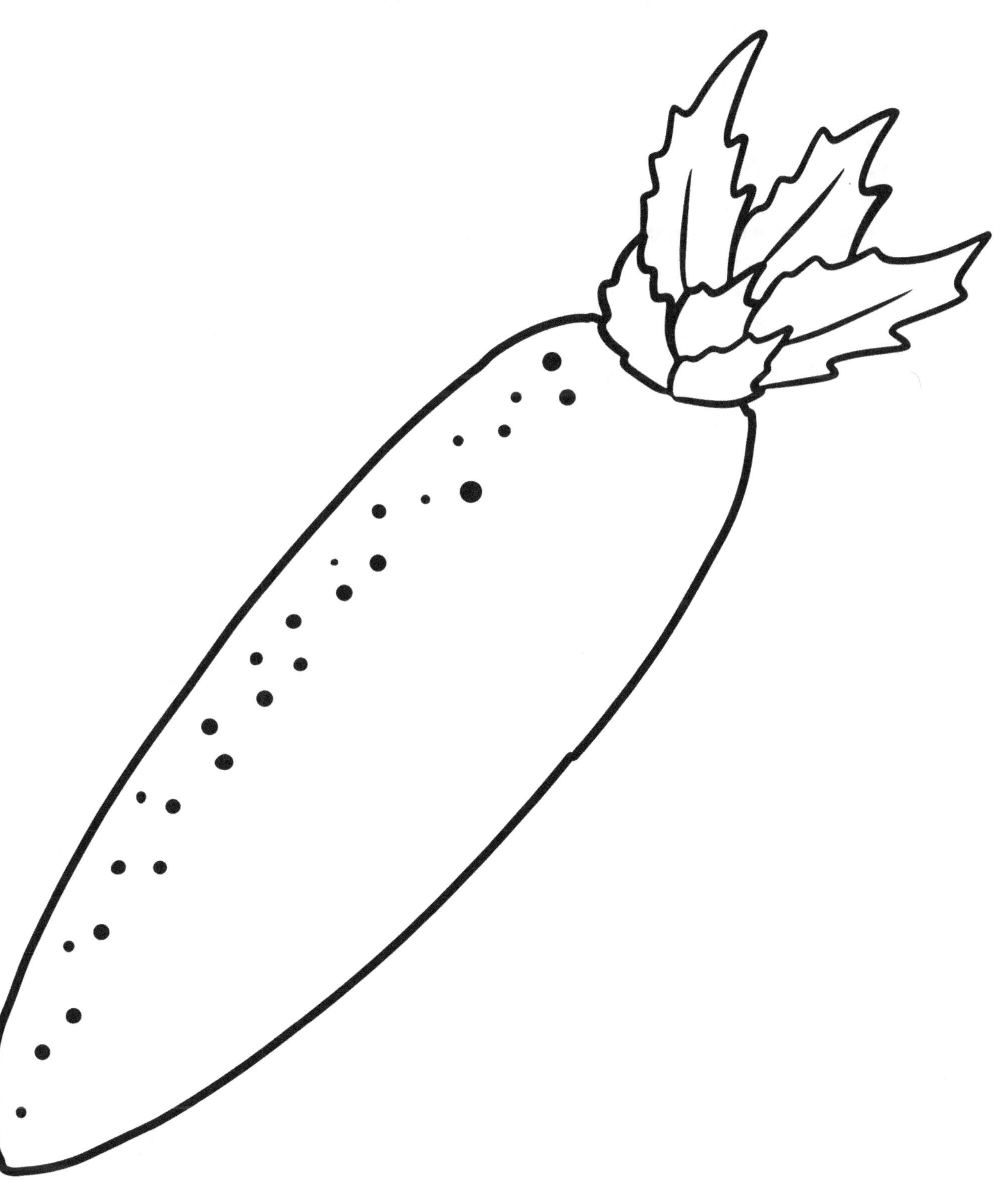

BELL PEPPER

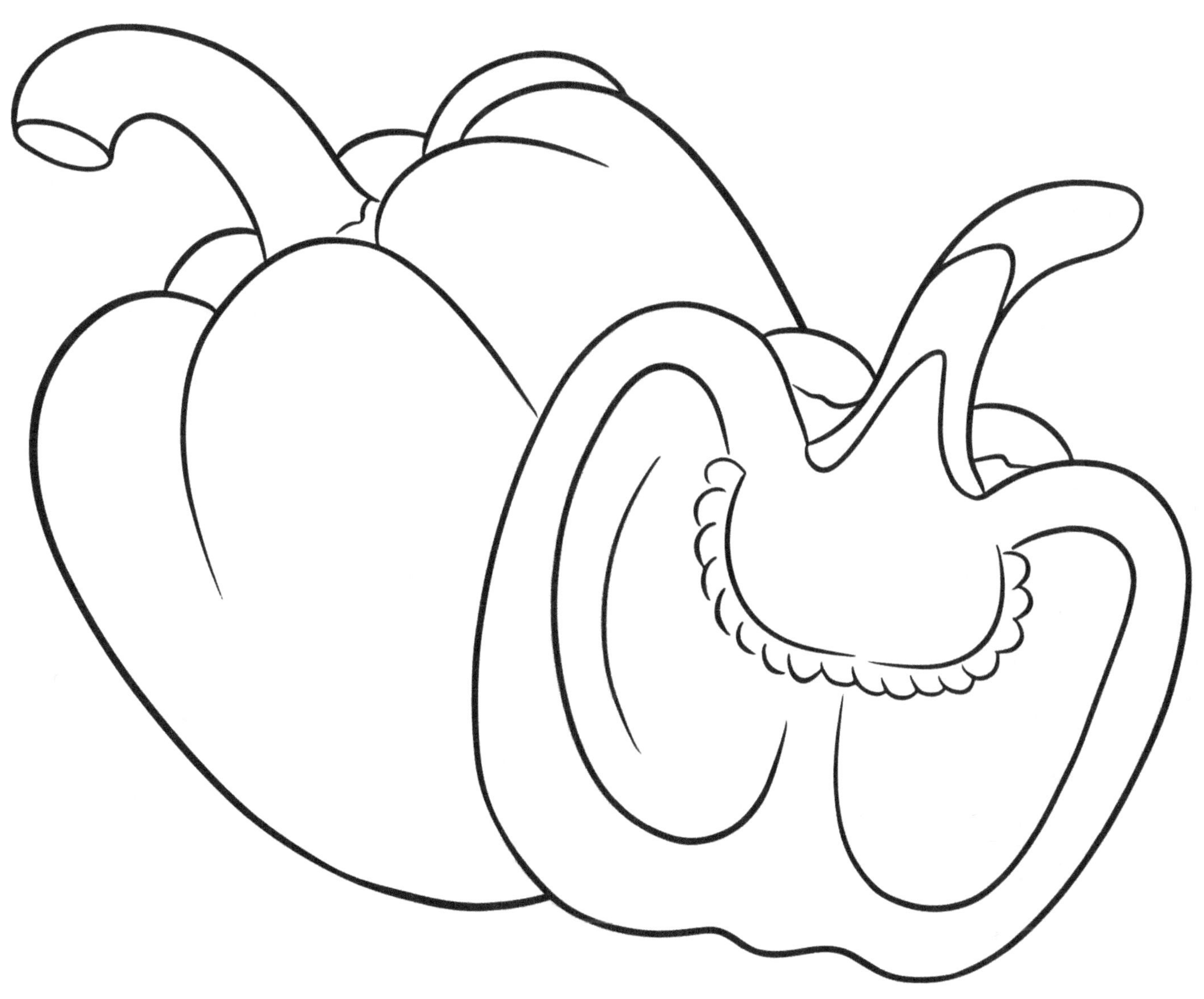

GINGER

PICKLE

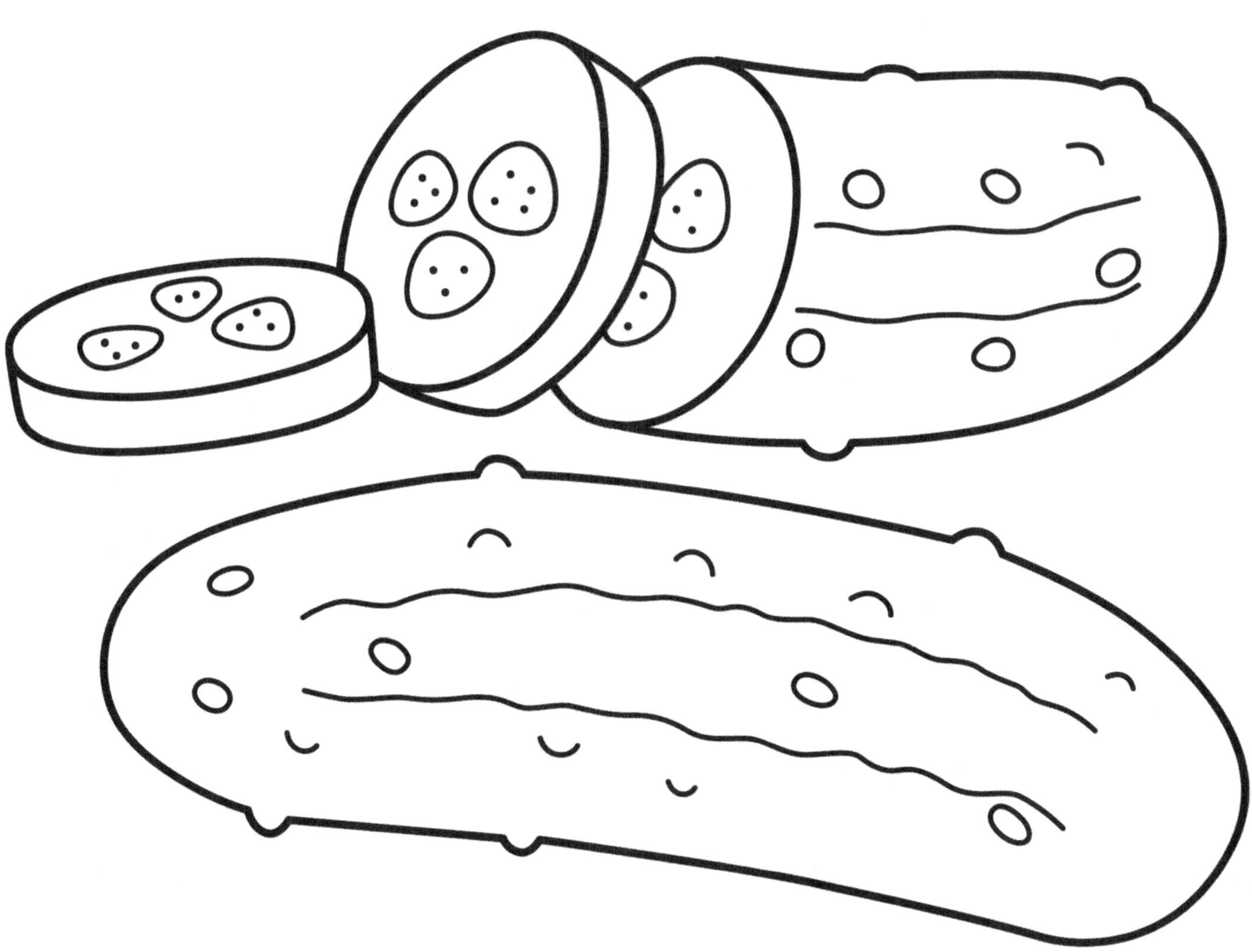

GARLIC

CARROT

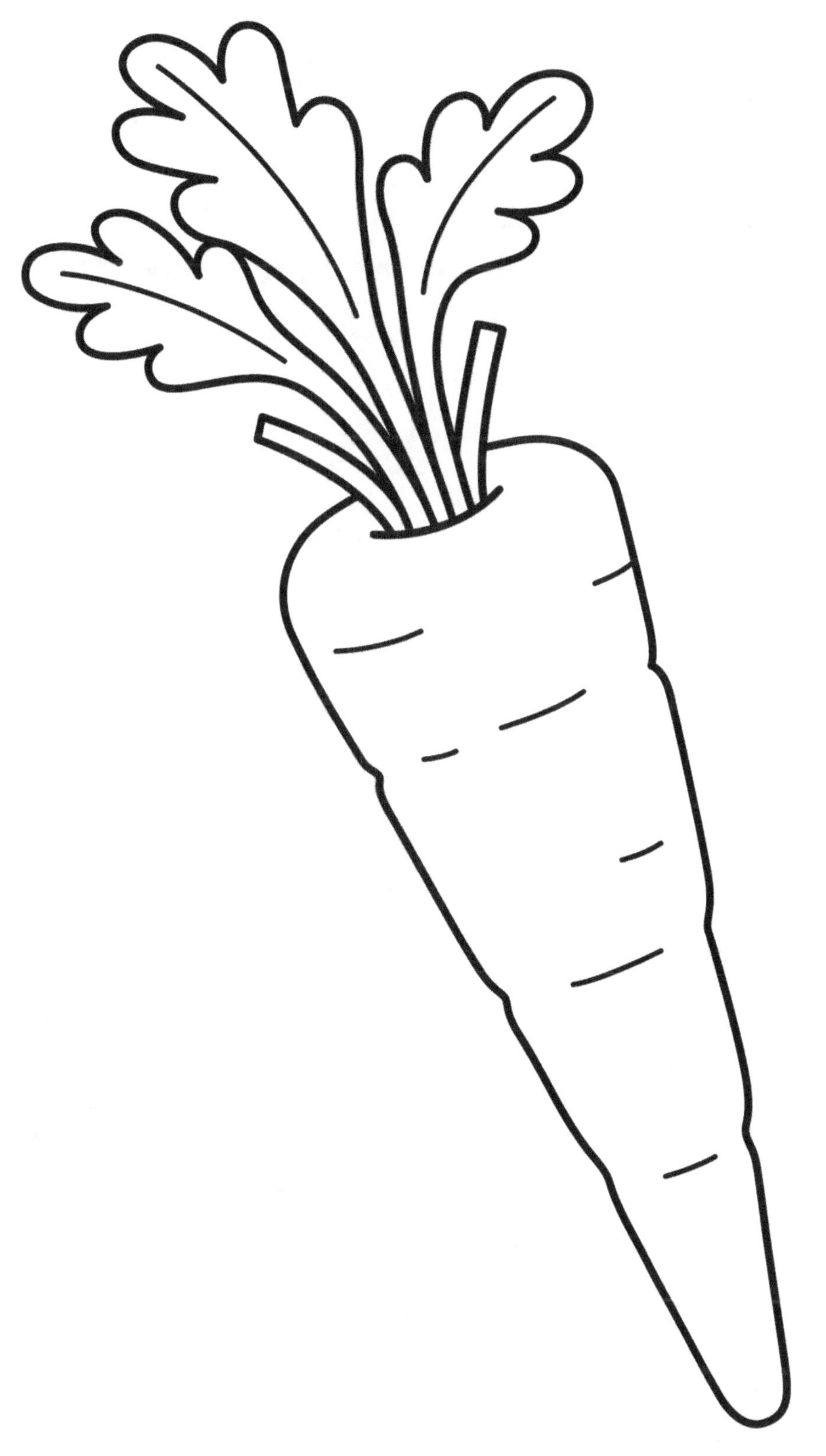

ASPARAGUS

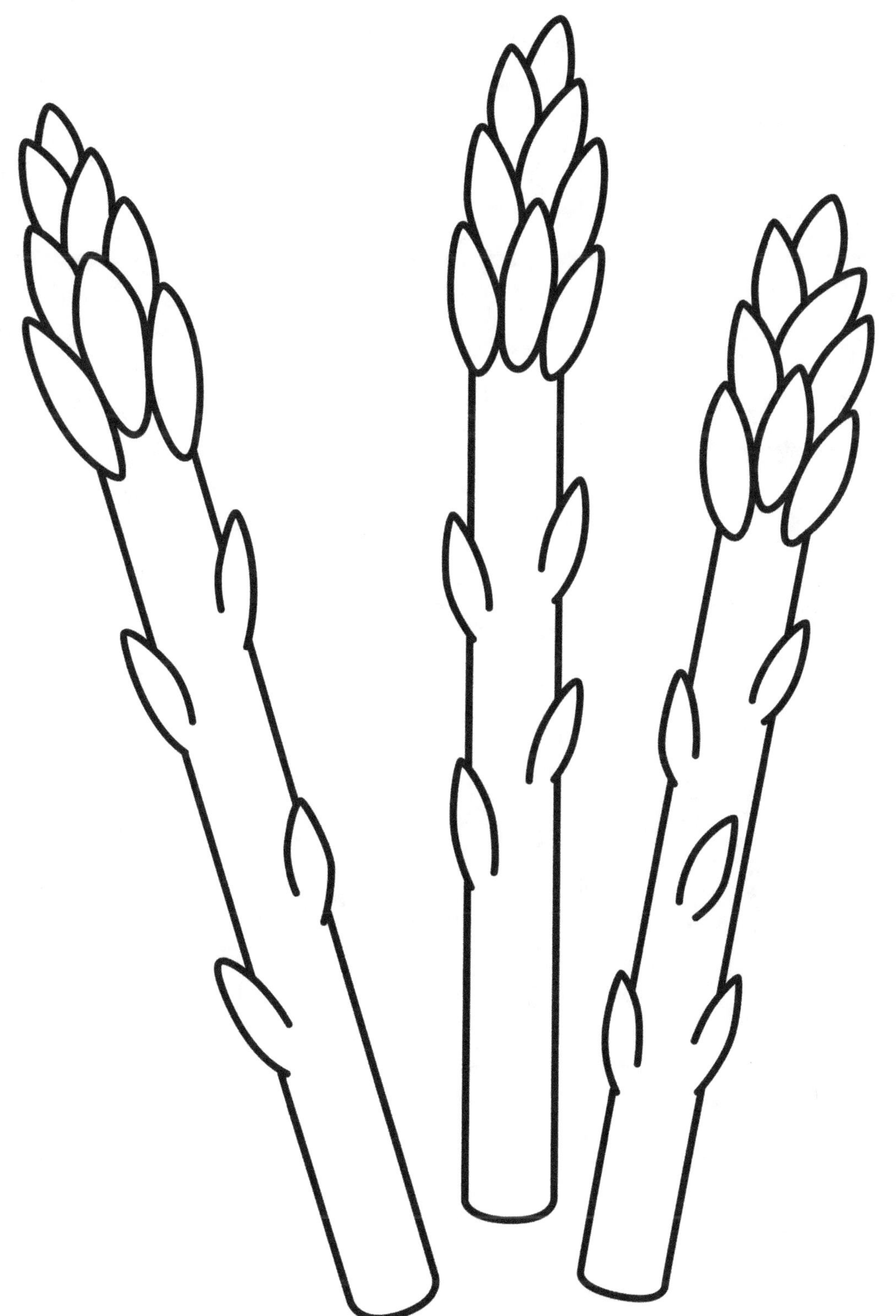

ONION

PUMPKIN

LETTUCE

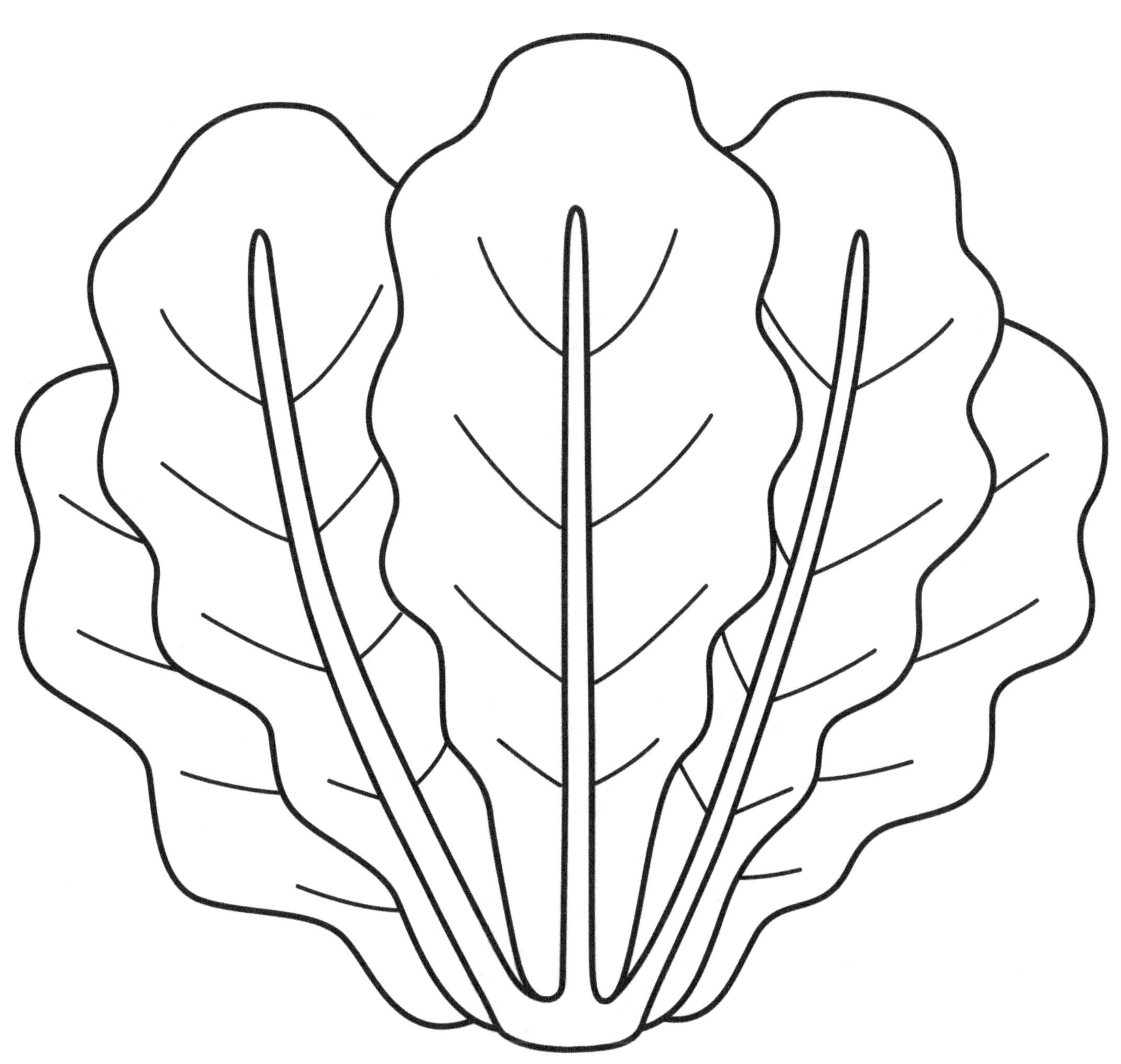

POTATO

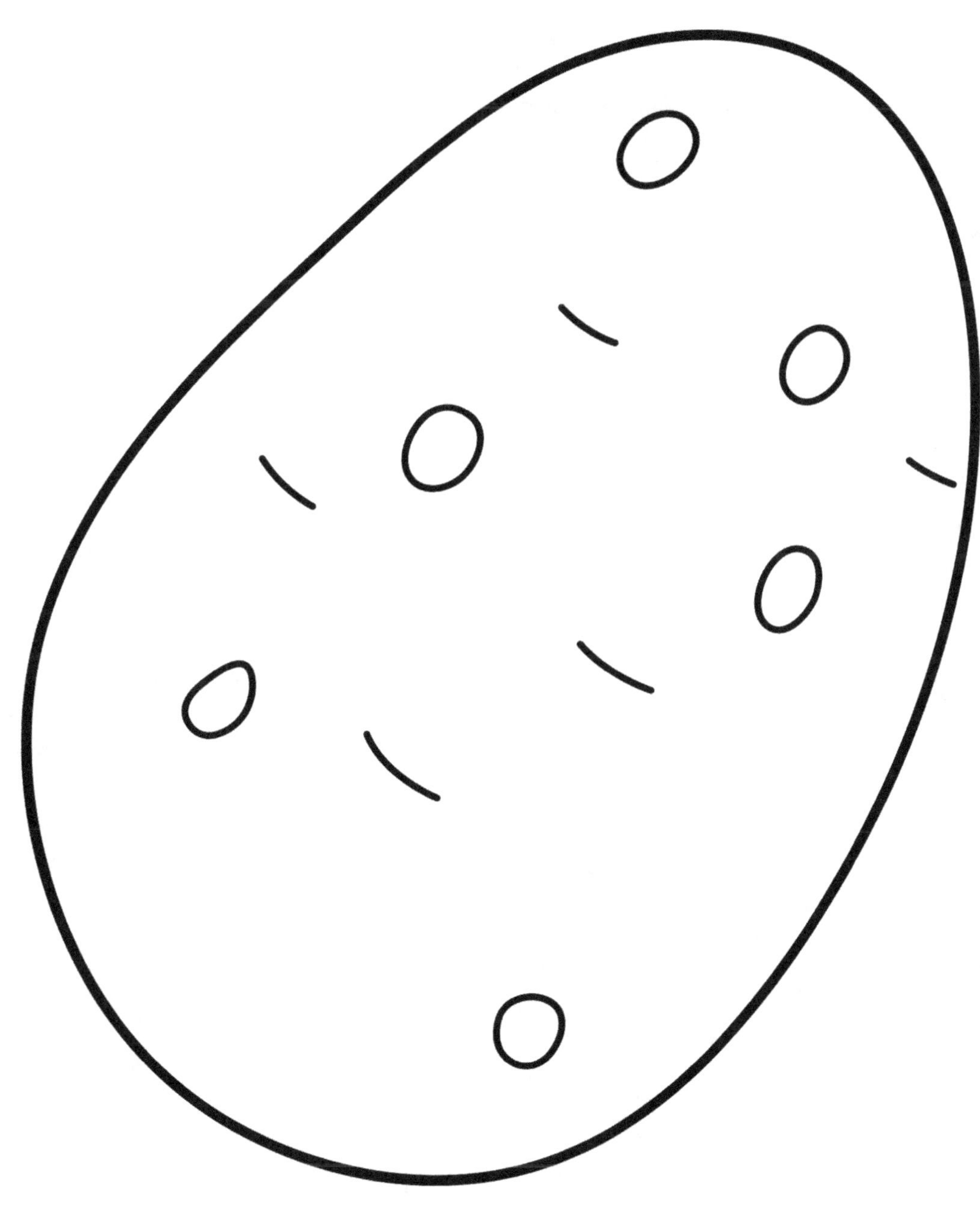

CAULI FLOWER

PEAS

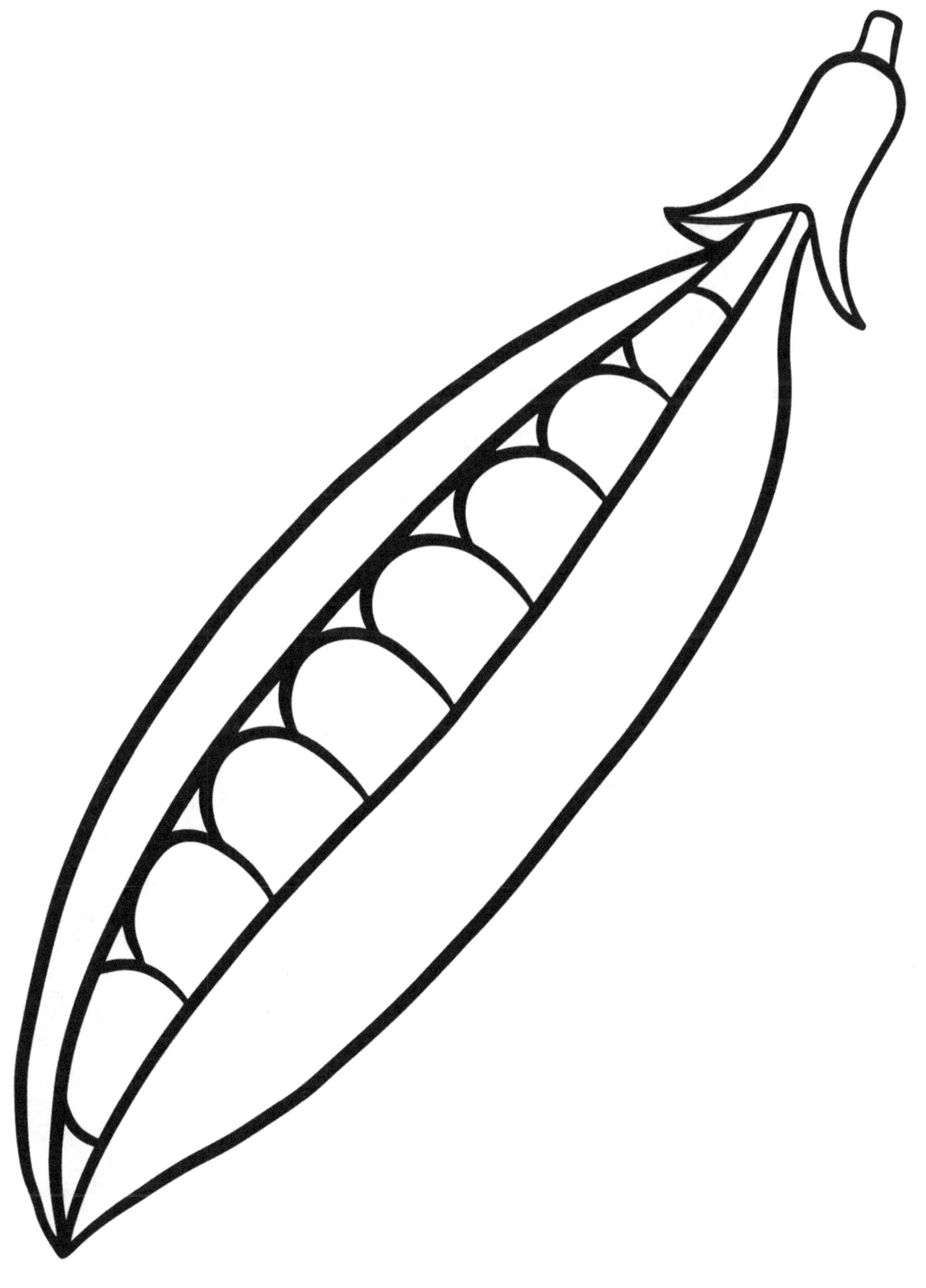

CORN

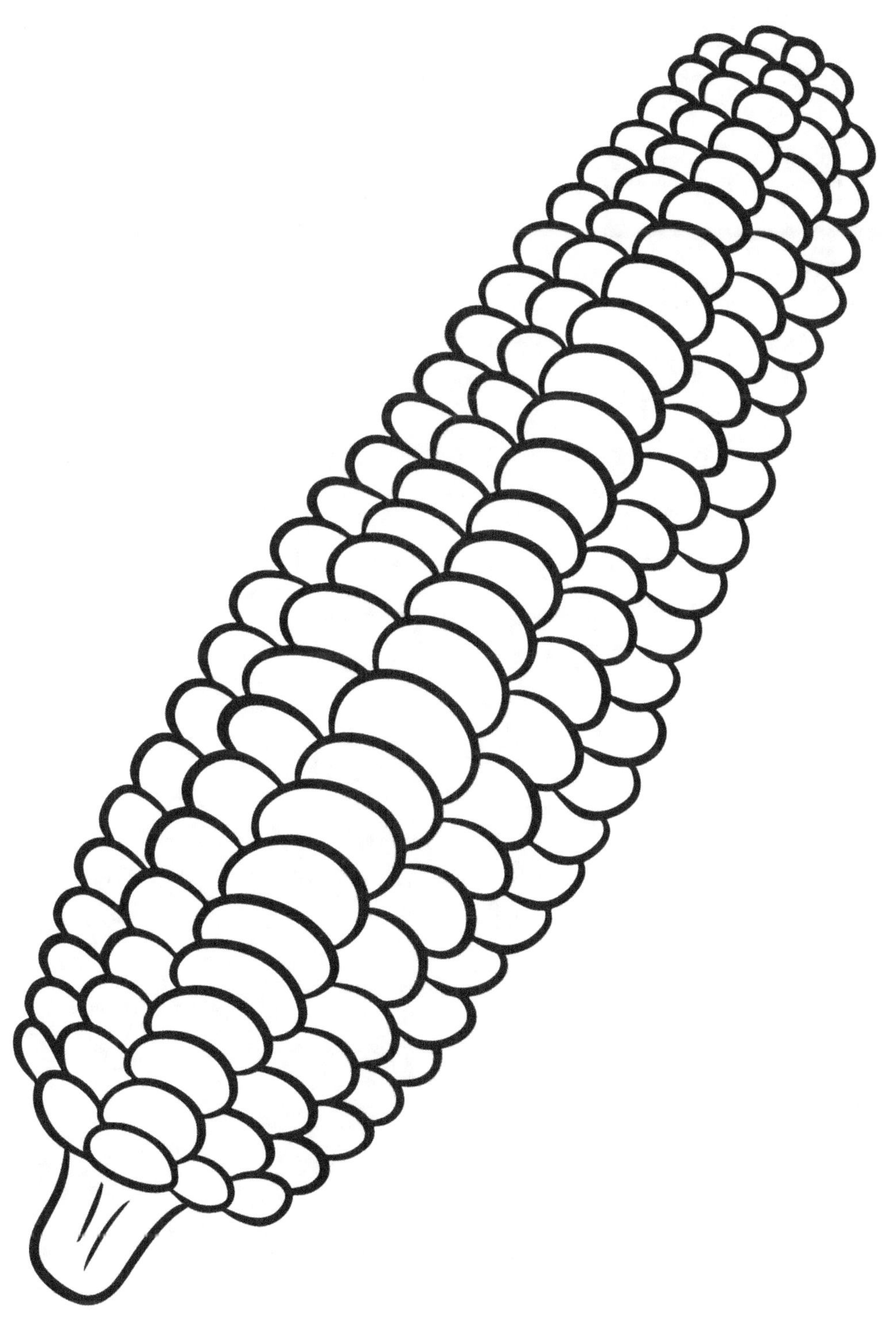

ZUCCHINI

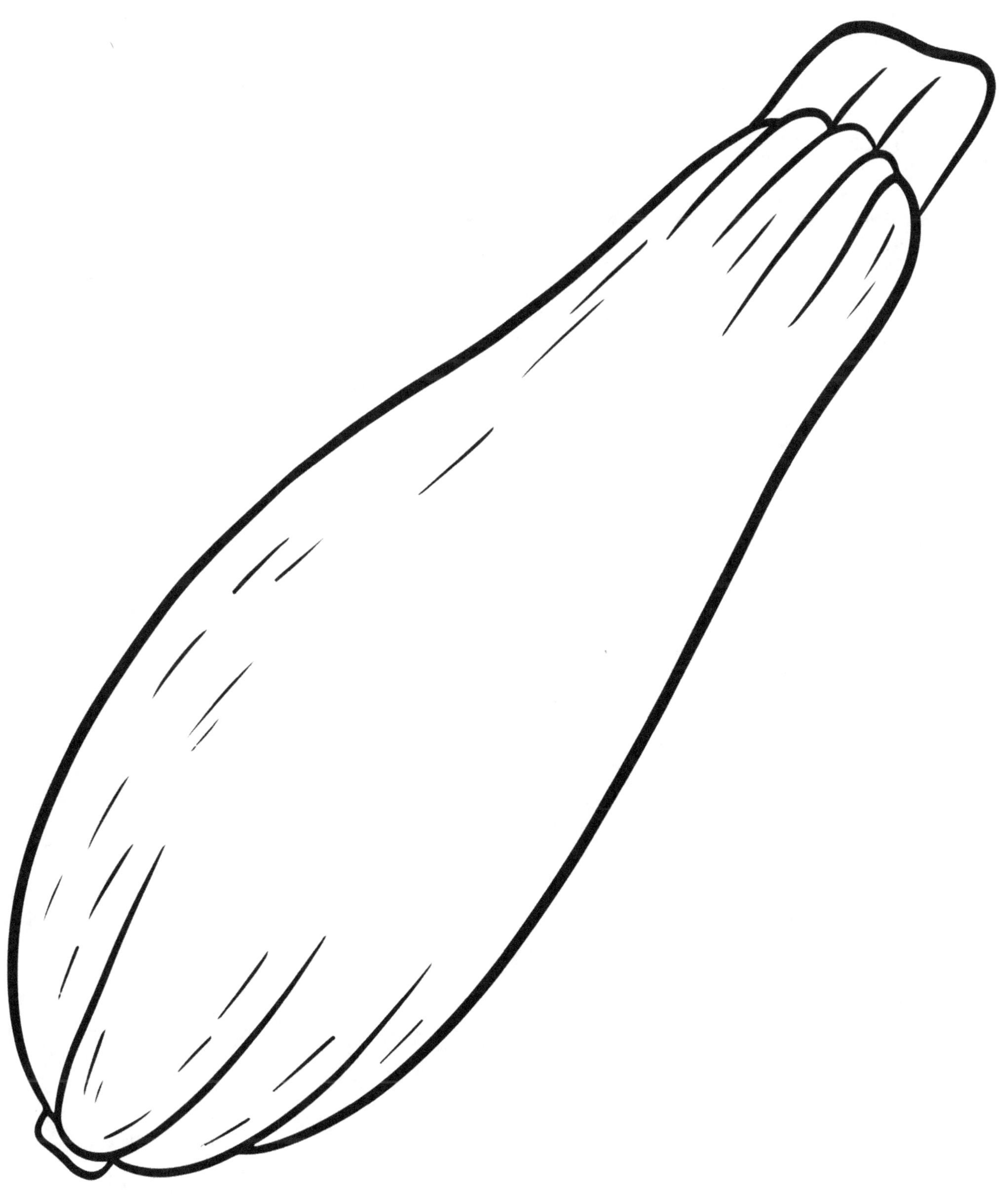

SPRING ONION

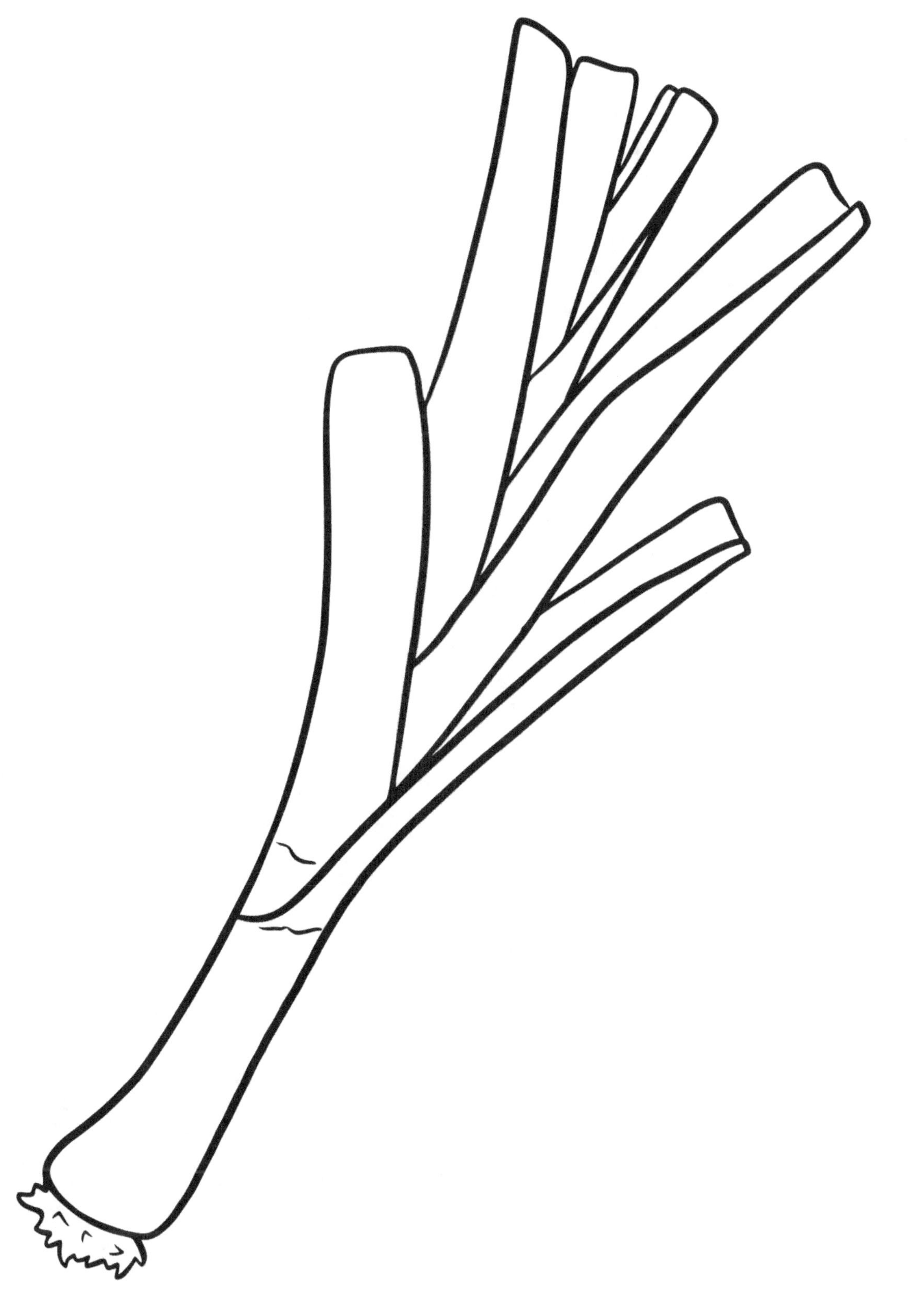

GREEN CHICKPEAS

GREEN BEANS

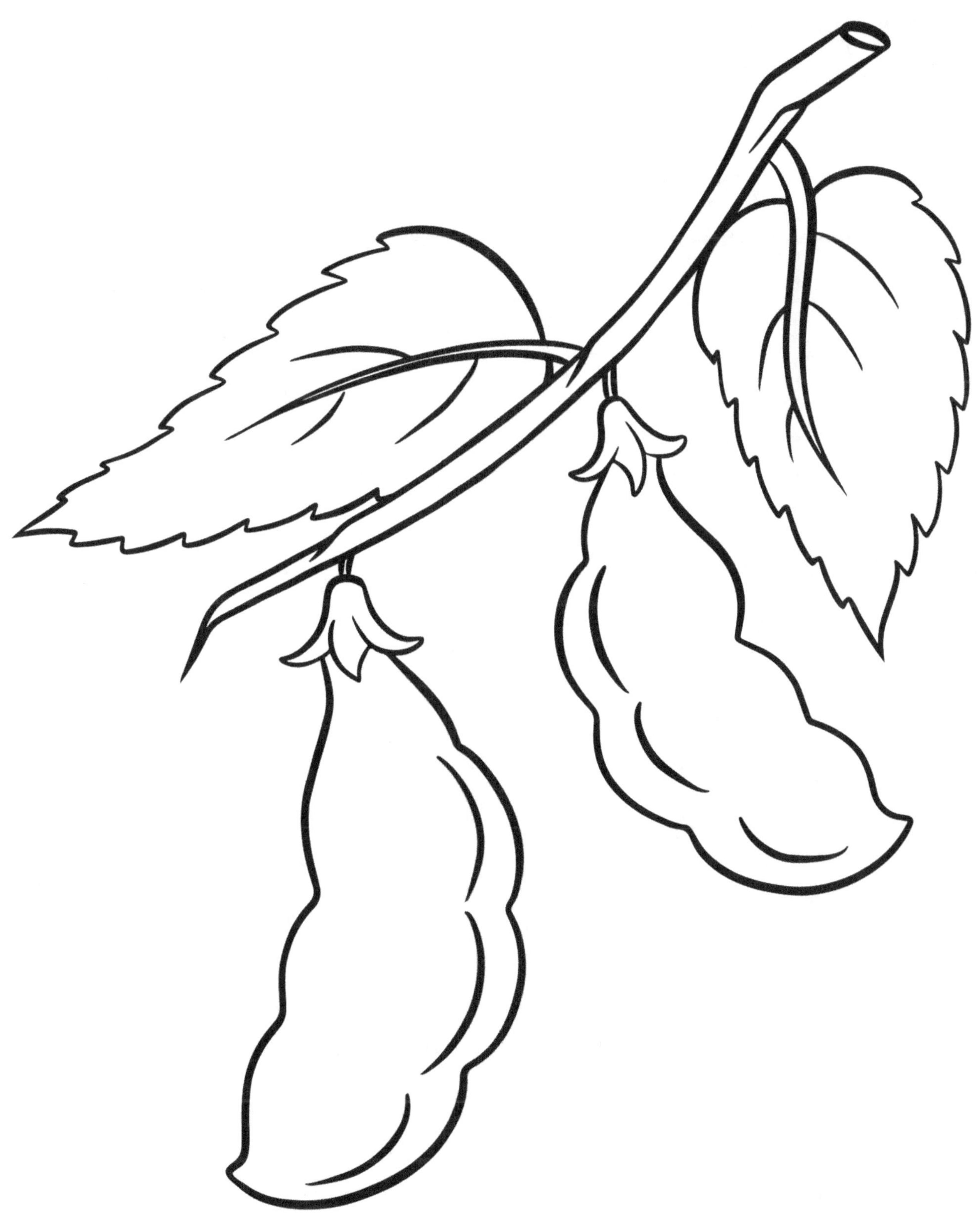

RED BEANS

MUSHROOM

RADISH

BEET ROOT

BITTER GOURD

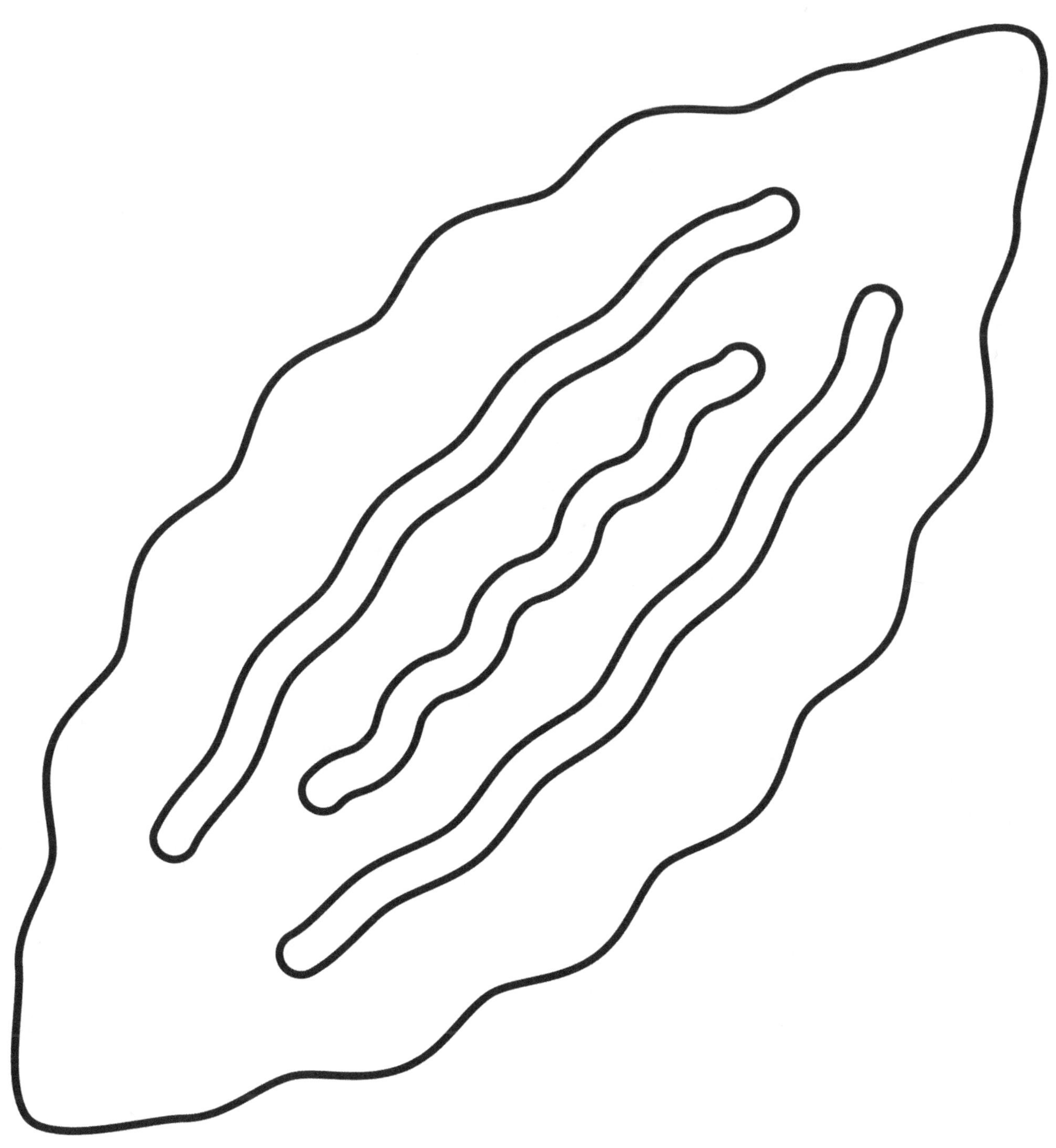

BOK CHOY

CELERY

CORIANDER

LADY FINGER

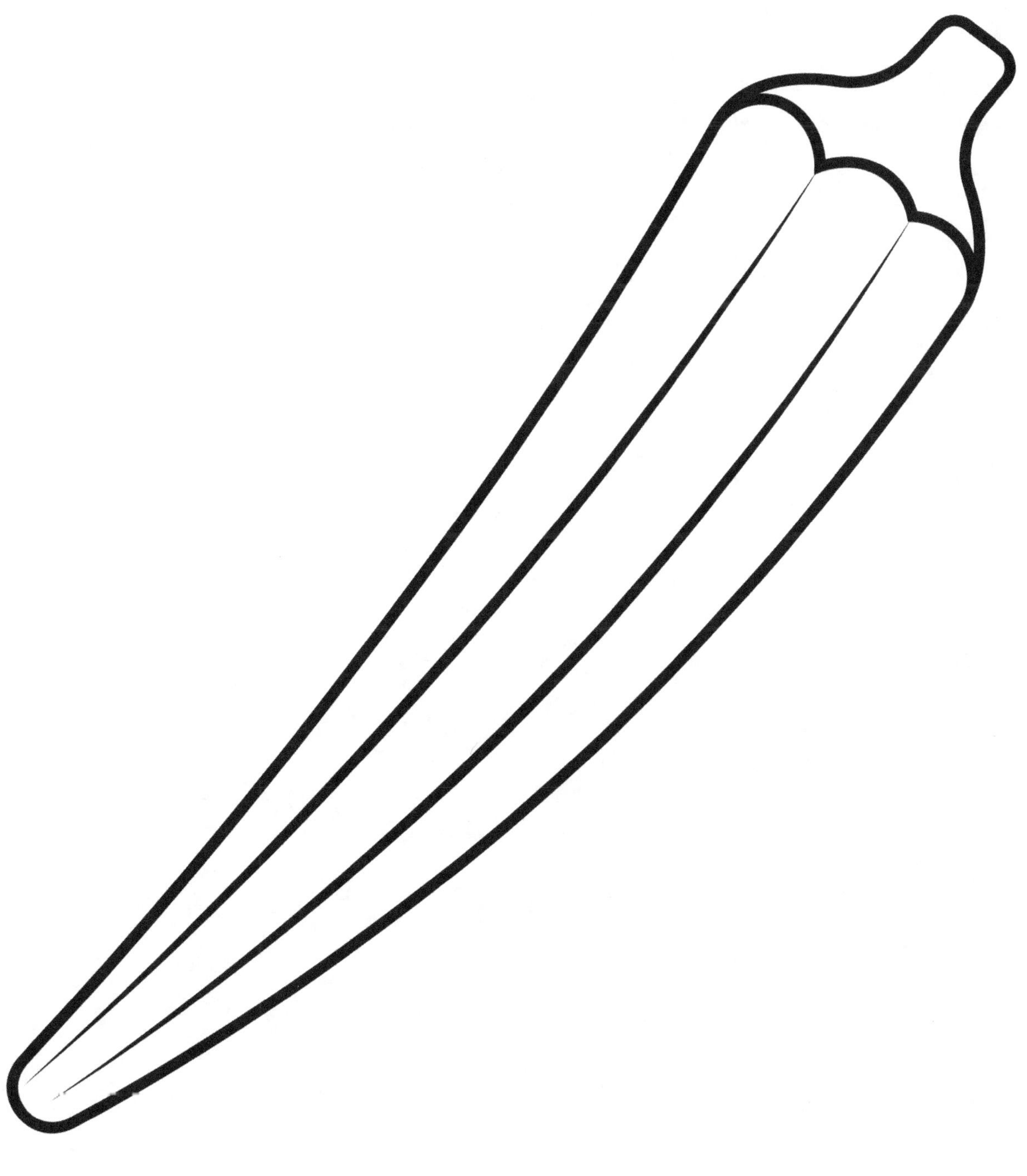

MINT

SPINACH

LEEK

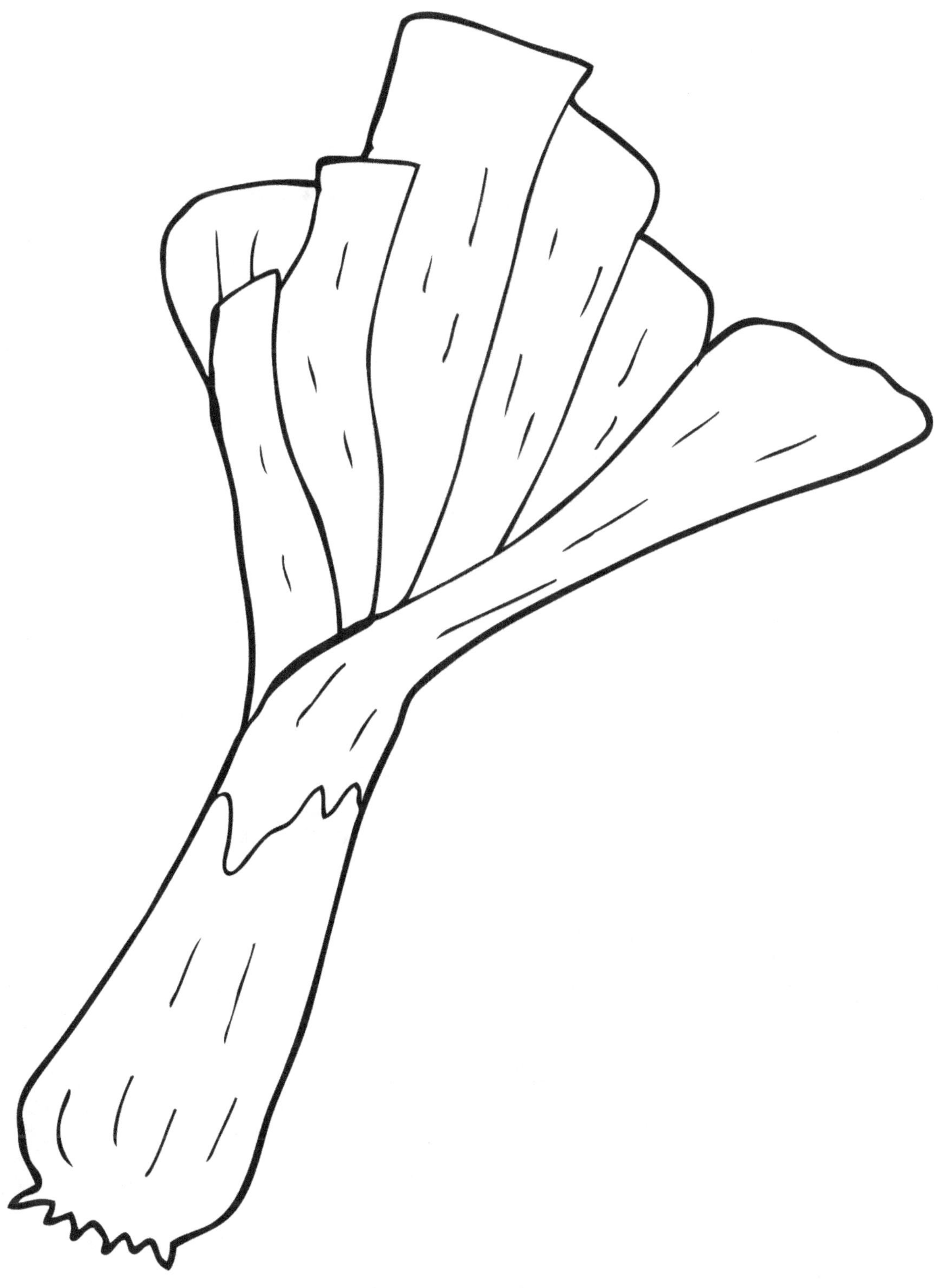

KALE

BOTTLE GOURD